50 NAMES YOU NEED TO KNOW!

WHO'S WHO IN...

EXPLORATION

ANITA GANERI

Published 2008 by
A & C Black Publishers Ltd.
38 Soho Square, London, W1D 3HB
www.acblack.com

Hardback ISBN 978-1-4081-0429-3

Paperback ISBN 978-1-4081-1091-1

Every effort has been made to trace copyright holders and to obtain their permission for use of copyright material. The authors and publishers would be pleased to rectify any error or omission in future editions.

This book is produced using paper that is made from wood grown in managed, sustainable forests. It is natural, renewable and recyclable. The logging and manufacturing processes conform to the environmental regulations of the country of origin.

Printed and bound in China by WKT.

All the internet addresses given in this book were correct at the time of going to press. The author and publishers regret any inconvenience caused if addresses have changed or sites have ceased to exist, but can accept no responsibility for any such changes.

Acknowledgements
The publishers would like to thank the following for their kind permission to reproduce their photographs:
Cover image: Underwood & Underwood/CORBIS Pages: 4 The Ancient Art & Architecture Collection Ltd; 5 The Ancient Art & Architecture Collection Ltd; 6 Bettman / Corbis; 7 Hulton-Deutsch Collection/CORBIS; 8 The Ancient Art & Architecture Collection Ltd; 9 Chris Hellier/Corbis; 10 PoodlesRock/Corbis; 11 Stefano Bianchetti/Corbis; 12 Library of Congress Prints and Photographs; 13 Bettmann/CORBIS; 14 Hulton-Deutsch Collection/CORBIS; 15 Bettmann/CORBIS; Reuters/CORBIS; 16 Bettmann/CORBIS; Gravure du XVIIIe siècle; 17 Stefano Bianchetti/CORBIS; 18 Bettmann/CORBIS; 19 Bettmann/CORBIS; 20 Bettmann/CORBIS; 21 Time & Life Pictures/Getty Images; 22 Amelie Legrand de Saint-Aubin; 23 Hulton-Deutsch Collection/CORBIS; 24 Chris Hellier/CORBIS; 25 Hulton-Deutsch Collection/CORBIS; 26 Hulton-Deutsch Collection/CORBIS; 27 Getty Images; Joanna Vestey/Corbis; 28 Ludovic Maisant/CORBIS; Getty Images; 29 Bettmann/CORBIS; 30 Time & Life Pictures/Getty Images; 31 Hulton-Deutsch Collection/CORBIS; 32 Mukunda Bogati/ZUMA/Corbis; Galen Rowell/CORBIS; 33 Bettmann/CORBIS; 34 Bettmann/CORBIS; 35 Bettmann/CORBIS; 36 Bettmann/CORBIS; 37 CORBIS; 38 Hulton-Deutsch Collection/CORBIS; 39 Underwood & Underwood/CORBIS; 40 Bettmann/CORBIS; 41 Bettmann/CORBIS; 42 Bettmann/CORBIS; 43 Bettmann/CORBIS; 44 CORBIS; 45 Joanna Vestey/Corbis

Contents

Hanno of Carthage

A daring explorer from Carthage, the greatest **trading** city in the ancient Mediterranean, Hanno led a fleet on one of the most remarkable voyages of ancient times.

An African voyage

Hanno set off from Carthage in North Africa and sailed down the west coast of Africa. His mission was to set up **colonies** to guard the Carthaginians' trade routes. Along his route he met hippos and hairy "people" (probably chimpanzees).

Find out more

Discover more about Hanno's amazing voyages at:
http://phoenicia.org/proutes.html

Timeline

Born in Carthage

Carthage is destroyed by the Romans

c. 814 BC   c. **late 7th century BC**   c. **early 6th century BC**   **146 BC**

Founding of Carthage in North Africa

Leads fleet down the west coast of Africa

Pytheas the Greek

Pytheas was a great explorer, geographer and **astronomer** from Ancient Greece. In the 4th century BC, he set sail from Marseilles, France, to explore northern Europe, at the very edge of the known world.

Journey north

Pytheas sailed north from Greece up the west coast of France. Crossing the Atlantic Ocean, he sailed around Britain to a place called Thule (probably Norway).

Find out more

Read about Pytheas the Greek's incredible journeys: "The Extraordinary Voyage of Pytheas the Greek" by Barry Cunliffe

Timeline

Born in Marseilles, France (a Greek colony)

Writes a book about his journey, called On the Ocean

c. 380 BC   c. **325 BC**   c. **320 BC**   c. **310 BC**

Makes journey to north-west Europe

Dies (place unknown)

Hsuan Tsang (Xuanzang)

Hsuan Tsang was a Buddhist monk from China. He became famous for his epic overland journey to India to visit the sacred sites of Buddhism and study Buddhist texts.

Early life

Hsuan Tsang was the youngest of four children. From an early age, he was interested in Buddhism – a way of life based on the teachings of a man known as the Buddha. Tsang spent many years studying in monasteries, eventually becoming a monk when he was 20 years old.

What he said

66 I will allow you to take my life, but I will not take a single step backwards in the direction of China. 99

Timeline

Born in China — Sets out to travel to India — Completes his account of his travels

C. **602**   C. **622**   C. **629**   C. **645**   C. **646**   C. **664**

Becomes a Buddhist monk — Returns to China — Dies in China

Find out more

Follow Tsang's journey to India at:
www.tzuchi.org/global/silkroad/

Find out more about Tsang's life at:
www.historyforkids.org/learn/china/religion/hsuantsang.htm

Read an in-depth account of Tsang's life:
www.biographybase.com/biography/Xuan_Zang.html

Pilgrimage to India

In AD 629, legend says Hsuan Tsang had a dream encouraging him to make the long, hard **pilgrimage** to India, the birthplace of Buddhism. Foreign travel was banned at that time, so Tsang left China in secret. He had to cross the Gobi Desert, nearly dying of thirst when he lost his water supplies.

He finally reached India in 630, after a journey filled with danger. He then spent many years visiting monasteries and sites associated with the Buddha's life.

When Tsang returned to China in 645, he brought more than 650 sacred Buddhist texts with him, together with hundreds of religious objects.

Did you know?

When Tsang died, the Chinese emperor cancelled his audiences for three days.

Erik the Red

Nicknamed for the colour of his hair, daring Viking explorer, Erik the Red, built the first European settlement on the island of Greenland.

What he said

66 People will desire much the more to go there if the land [Greenland] has a good name. 99

How did he die?

Erik the Red died from a disease brought to Greenland by a new wave of settlers from Iceland.

Viking voyages

In the late 8th century, Vikings from Scandinavia made incredible voyages. Viking settlements in Scandinavia had become very overcrowded, so the Vikings set sail for new lands to settle, covering vast distances as they travelled.

Timeline

Born in Norway	Outlawed from Iceland; explores Greenland	Establishes settlements on Greenland	Son, Leif, explores North America	Dies in Greenland
c. 950	c. 982	c. 985	c. 1002	c. 1003

Erik the Red's story

Erik's father had settled in Iceland with his family. Some years later, Erik the Red was **outlawed** for murder and banished from Iceland for three years. During this time, Erik sailed west in search of a mysterious island sighted many years earlier.

Settling in Greenland

Back in Iceland, Erik told stories about the island, which he named "Greenland" because he thought it would sound appealing. In 985, Erik sailed back to Greenland with a large number of ships and many settlers. Under Erik's leadership, the Vikings established two settlements on the south-west coast, one of which lasted until the 16th century.

Marco Polo

One of the first Europeans to explore China, Marco Polo travelled widely, finding places unknown in Europe at that time.

A merchant family

Polo's father, Niccolo, and uncle, Maffeo, were wealthy jewel **merchants** who travelled the world to buy and sell jewels. Niccolo and Maffeo had already made the long journey to China, along trade routes through Central Asia. In China, they were welcomed by Kublai Khan, the emperor of the **Mongols** who ruled China at the time.

Travelling east

In 1271, Niccolo and Maffeo set off again. This time, they took 16-year-old Marco Polo with them. It was a long and treacherous journey, crossing mountain ranges and bone-dry deserts. They finally reached Kublai Khan's summer palace at Shangdu in May 1275, three and a half years after setting out. Marco Polo spent 17 years travelling all over China on Kublai Khan's behalf.

What he said

❝ I have not told half of what I saw because no one would have believed me. ❞

How did he die?

Marco Polo died at home in Venice in 1324 or 1325. He was 70 years old.

Timeline

1254	1271	1275	1292	1298	1324 or 1325
Born in Venice, Italy, on 15 September		Reaches Kublai Khan's summer palace in China		Taken prisoner by the Genoese	
	Travels to China		Sails from China for home		Dies in Venice

Find out more

To read more about his life, search for Marco Polo at: www.silkroadfoundation.org

Find out more about Marco Polo at: www.cdli.ca/CITE/expolo.htm

The Polos left China in 1292 and reached Venice three years later. Soon afterwards, Marco Polo was taken prisoner by the Genoese who were at war with Venice. In prison, he told the story of his travels to a fellow prisoner called Rusticello, who wrote it down. The account was called *Il Milione* ("The Million") and became a bestseller.

Ibn Battuta

During his lifetime, explorer Ibn Battuta travelled an astonishing 120,000 kilometres (74,500 miles), covering most of the Muslim world and beyond.

What he said

66 The hens in China are bigger than geese in our country. 99

How did he die?

Battuta died of Black Death, which swept across North Africa and the Middle East.

Traveller of Islam

Battuta was born in Tangier, Morocco. He was a Muslim (a follower of the religion of Islam). After he completed his law studies, he set off on a pilgrimage to the holy city of **Makkah** in Saudi Arabia. This journey marked the beginning of 30 years of travelling. Battuta vowed never to travel the same road twice (except when visiting Makkah).

Timeline

Born on 24 February in Tangier	Made a judge in India	Arrives home to Tangier	Dies in Tangier
1304	c. 1325	c. 1333	c. 1354	c. 1360	c. 1377
	Visits Makkah for the first time		Dictates the *Rihla*, an account of his travels	

Find out more

Read an in-depth account about Battuta at:
www.saudiaramcoworld.com/issue/200004/the.longest.hajj.the.journeys.of.ibn.battuta-editor.s.note.htm

Read Battuta's own account of his travels:
www.fordham.edu/halsall/source/1354-ibnbattuta.html

Take a virtual tour of the places Battuta explored at:
www.sfusd.k12.ca.us/schwww/sch618/Ibn_Battuta/Ibn_Battuta_Rihla.html

Further journeys

On one of his great journeys, Battuta set out for India. Battuta reached the court of the Muslim Sultan of Delhi in 1333. At first, the Sultan welcomed him and appointed him as a judge. Later, Battuta fell out of favour and had to flee to China to save his life.

Almost 25 years after leaving Tangier, Battuta returned home. However, he could not give up his love of travel and was soon on the move again. His last great journey took him across the Sahara Desert to the famous city of Timbuktu. Battuta finally reached home in 1354, his amazing travels at an end.

Zheng He

China's greatest sailor, Admiral Zheng He, was chosen by the emperor to lead a fleet of huge treasure ships on a series of seven astonishing voyages around the world.

Emperor's orders

Born into a Muslim family, Zheng He grew up in Yunnan Province, China. In 1381, he was captured by the **imperial** army and sent to serve in the emperor's court. Zheng He soon became the emperor's favourite, and was asked to represent China in other countries. In 1405, Emperor Yong Le put him in charge of a fleet of about 300 ships with a crew of as many as 28,000 men.

Did you know?

Chinese treasure ships could carry 500 passengers and huge amounts of goods.

Timeline

Born in Yunnan Province, China		Dies on final voyage	
1371	1405–22	1430–33	1433
	Six voyages	Seventh voyage	

Find out more

Take a look at the instruments Zheng He used to navigate:
www.dragonvoyage.com/kids-zone/navigation.shtml

Find out more about Zheng He and China:
www.asiarecipe.com/chicheng.html

Seven voyages

On his first three voyages, Zheng He reached south-east Asia, India, and Sri Lanka. His huge fleet included many nine-masted "treasure ships", which were the largest ships in the world.

On his fourth voyage, Zheng He sailed across the Arabian Sea as far as Arabia and the Persian Gulf. His voyages added greatly to Chinese knowledge of the world. However, when Emperor Yong Le died in 1424, the new rulers banned foreign travel and trade. Zheng He had already fallen out of favour with the new rulers but he made one last voyage. Most of the records of his voyages were later destroyed.

How did he die?

It is thought that Zheng He died during his last voyage and was buried at sea.

Christopher Columbus

In 1492, Italian sailor Christopher Columbus set sail across the Atlantic Ocean on an extraordinary voyag[e]. He hoped to find a new trade route to the riches of Asia. Instead, he discovered a whole new world.

What he said

66 Martin Alonzon called out with great joy that he saw land, and demanded of the Admiral a reward. 99

How did he die?

Columbus died from an unknown illness when he was 55 years old.

Early life

Columbus was fascinated by the sea. While working in Lisbon, Portugal, he came up with the plan of reaching Asia by sailing west. However, he first needed to find wealthy people to fund his voyage.

Timeline

1451	1492	1493–96	1498–1500	1502–04	1506

Born in Genoa, Italy — 1451

Sets sail on first voyage across the Atlantic — 1492

Second voyage — 1493–96

Third voyage — 1498–1500

Fourth voyage — 1502–04

Dies in Valladolid, Spain, on 20 May — 1506

Eventually, the Spanish king and queen agreed to help him. With three ships – the *Santa María*, the *Niña*, and the *Pinta* – Columbus set sail in August 1492.

Across the Atlantic

After a dreadful voyage, Columbus spotted land. He stepped ashore on an island in the Bahamas in the Caribbean. He had reached a part of the world which no one in Europe knew existed. He called it the "New World".

Three more voyages followed. Columbus explored more of the West Indies and claimed Hispaniola (now called the Dominican Republic) for Spain. He did not govern the new lands well and was sent back to Spain in disgrace. He was later forgiven and allowed to sail on one last voyage – to the South American mainland.

Vasco da Gama

Six years after Columbus's first voyage, Portuguese navigator Vasco da Gama became the first European to sail around Africa and reach India by sea.

Early life

Da Gama came from a family of soldiers. His father was a knight who served the King of Portugal's son. It seems that Vasco da Gama followed in his father's footsteps and became a tough soldier. He also studied **navigation** and, in 1497, was chosen by the king to command an expedition. His mission was to find a new trade route to India by sailing around Africa and into the unknown.

What he said

66 The women [of Calicut]… wear many jewels of gold round the neck. 99

How did he die?

Da Gama died in India of the disease **malaria** on 24 December 1524.

Timeline

Born in Sines, Portugal	Reaches Calicut in India in May		Returns to India	
c. **1469**	**1497**	**1498**	**1502–04**	**1524** **1524**
	Sets sail for India on 8 July	Second voyage to India	Dies in Kochi, India	

Find out more

Lots more detail about da Gama's life and travels can be found at: www.bbc.co.uk/history/british/tudors/vasco_da_gama_01.shtml

An easy-to-use site, with lots of information about da Gama: www.elizabethan-era.org.uk

Passage to India

On 8 July 1497, da Gama's fleet of four ships and 170 men set sail. Vasco da Gama boldly headed out into the South Atlantic Ocean to take advantage of the winds instead of staying near the coast. Sailing out of sight of land was risky but successful. In November, Vasco da Gama reached Africa. Finally, he set out across the Indian Ocean. With the help of an Indian **pilot**, the fleet reached Calicut, India, in May 1498.

Ferdinand Magellan

Portuguese explorer Ferdinand Magellan gained lasting fame as the first person to lead an expedition to sail around the world.

What he said

66 The Church says the Earth is flat but I know that it is round. For I have seen the shadow on the moon... 99

How did he die?

Magellan was killed in the Philippines, in a battle between two of the islands.

Find out more

Discover more about Magellan at:
http://library.thinkquest.org/J002678F/magellan.htm

Lots of information about Magellan's life and travels can be found at:
www.esd.k12.ca.us/Matsumoto/TM30/history/Explorers/fmag.html

Early life

As a young boy, Magellan worked at the Portuguese court. He learned navigation and map-making — skills that would be vital later in his life. He also heard stories of daring voyages, such as Vasco da Gama's, that opened up trade routes to the East. Later, Magellan joined several of these expeditions, sailing east around Africa. He became convinced that he could reach the East by sailing west, around South America.

Timeline

Born in Sabrosa, Portugal	Leaves Portugal for Spain			Dies in Cebu, Philippines, on 27 April	
1480	**1505**	**1517**	**1519**	**1521**	**1522**
	Goes to sea for the first time		Sets sail from Spain		Juan Sebastian de Elcano leads the *Vittoria* back to Spain

Around the world

Magellan set sail in September 1519 with a fleet of five ships and around 270 men. A year after setting out, Magellan sailed through what is now the Magellan Straits (named after him) and into the Pacific Ocean. Crossing the vast Pacific was terrible and many men died of starvation and disease. In March 1521, Magellan finally reached the island of Guam, and then sailed on to the Philippines. There, Magellan was killed. Eighteen months later, the sole surviving ship, the *Vittoria*, sailed back to Spain. Of the original crew, only 18 men had survived the trip.

Sir Francis Drake

The second journey around the world was led by daring English sea captain, Sir Francis Drake. Nicknamed "the Dragon", his mission was to steal from Spanish treasure ships.

Treasure hunter

Drake first went to sea at the age of 12 when he was taken on as an **apprentice** on a small cargo ship. The ship was left to him when the captain died. A few years later, Drake made the first of several voyages to the New World (now the United States). Drake's mission was to seek out Spanish ships and steal all the treasure on board.

What he said

66 There is plenty of time to win this game, and to thrash the Spaniards, too. 99

Timeline

| 1541 or 1543 | 1563 | 1577 | 1581 | 1588 | 1596 |

- Born in Devon, England — 1541 or 1543
- Sails to the New World for the first time — 1563
- Sails around the world — 1577
- Knighted by Queen Elizabeth I — 1581
- Helps to defeat the Spanish Armada — 1588
- Dies in Central America in January — 1596

Find out more

Read about Drake's life and his achievements at:
www.spartacus.schoolnet.co.uk/TUDdrakeF.htm

Find out what Drake himself might have said about his life at:
http://library.thinkquest.org/J002678F/sir_francis_drake.htm

An epic voyage

In 1577, Drake was chosen by Queen Elizabeth I to command a voyage around the world. With five ships and 164 men, he set sail from Plymouth, looting Spanish ports and treasure ships on the way. Drake finally reached the west coast of the New World and claimed modern-day California for the Crown.

On 26 September 1580, Drake's ship, the *Golden Hind*, docked at Plymouth, loaded with gold and spices. Drake had sailed further up the west coast of the United States than any other European explorer. He also found open water to the south of South America, proving that it was not linked to another continent. Drake was knighted in honour of his achievements.

How did he die?

Drake died from **dysentery**. His body was buried at sea off the coast of Panama.

James Cook

The English sailor Captain James Cook made three daring voyages of discovery to find out what lay in the South Pacific.

What he said

66 Ambition leads me not only further than any other man has been before me, but as far as I think it possible for man to go. 99

How did he die?

Cook was killed in Hawaii when fighting broke out over the theft of a boat.

Early life

Born in the port of Whitby, Cook learned to sail in small coal ships. He later joined the Royal Navy and quickly gained promotion through the ranks. Then, in 1768, he led a new, scientific expedition to the island of Tahiti in the South Pacific.

Timeline

1728	1768–71	1772–75	1776–79	1779
Born in Yorkshire, England	First voyage to Tahiti	Second voyage to Antarctica	Third voyage to Hawaii	Dies in Hawaii on 14 February

Three voyages

On his first voyage, Cook travelled to Tahiti to observe the passage of the planet Venus in front of the Sun. His second voyage was to find the southern continent (**Antarctica**). Sailing south, Cook charted the coasts of New Zealand and Australia, but did not find the southern continent of Antarctica. Before he could reach the continent, his ship was forced back by sea ice. Cook's final voyage took him north to Hawaii and the west coast of North America.

Although Cook did not see Antarctica, his voyages covered huge areas of the Pacific Ocean that had never appeared on European maps before. The scientists he took with him brought back detailed information about the new and extraordinary places they visited.

Jacques Cousteau

Jacques Cousteau helped to develop the **aqualung**, a piece of equipment that revolutionized diving.

Underwater world

Cousteau joined the French Navy in 1930. In 1942, he developed the aqualung (underwater breathing equipment) with engineer Emile Gagnan. In 1950, Cousteau turned his research ship, *Calypso*, into a laboratory for diving and filming. He went on to make many TV programmes.

Find out more

The Cousteau Society's fun site is full of games and facts: www.cousteaukids.org/

Find out how scuba diving equipment works at: http://travel.howstuffworks.com/scuba.htm

Timeline

Born in France on 11 June

Sets up the Cousteau Society for the Protection of Ocean Life

1910   **1942**   **1973**   **1997**

Co-develops the aqualung

Dies in France on 25 June

Thor Heyerdahl

Norwegian scientist Thor Heyerdahl became famous for his epic voyages in flimsy boats across the Pacific and Atlantic Oceans.

Voyages into the past

Thousands of years ago, the Polynesians sailed from South America to the Pacific Islands and settled there. To prove this, Heyerdahl sailed a boat from Peru in South America to the Tuamoto Islands in the South Pacific.

Find out more

Discover more about Heyerdahl at: www.gonorway.no/go/heyerdahl.html

Another useful site: www.kontiki.no/Ny/Dok_eng/E-Heyerdahl.html

Timeline

Born in Norway on 6 October

Dies in Italy on 18 April

1914   **1947**   **2002**

Expedition to Tuamoto Islands

Robert Cavelier de La Salle

French trader Robert Cavelier de La Salle became famous for exploring the Great Lakes in northern USA and sailing all the way down the Mississippi River.

North American adventure

In 1669, La Salle led an expedition to the Ohio River. In 1679, he explored the Great Lakes and went on to canoe down the Mississippi River.

Find out more

Take a look at this virtual museum site:
www.civilization.ca/vmnf/
explor/lasal_e1.html

Timeline

1643	1666	1682	1687
Born in Rouen, France, on 22 November	Sails for Canada for the first time	Canoes down the Mississippi River	Murdered by his own men on 19 March

Charles Marie de La Condamine

French mathematician Charles Marie de la Condamine was a brilliant scientist. He was eager to travel to discover more about how the world works.

Expedition to South America

In 1735, La Condamine led an expedition to South America to settle an argument about the true shape and size of the Earth. He stayed on in South America, where he studied the plant and animal life of the tropical rainforest.

Timeline

1701	1735	1744	1751	1774
Born in Paris, France, on 28 January	Leads a scientific expedition to South America	Returns to France	Publishes an account of his travels	Dies on 4 February

Alexander von Humboldt

German scientist Alexander von Humboldt was one of the greatest scientific explorers of all. On his travels in South America, he discovered many species of animals and plants that had never been seen in Europe before.

Early life

Von Humboldt was born in Berlin (now in Germany), into a wealthy family. As a boy, he was fascinated by nature and spent his time collecting insects, plants, and shells. After university, he worked in the mining industry, during which time he invented a new safety lamp for miners.

What he said

66 Happiness depends more on the way we meet the events of life than on the nature of those events. 99

Timeline

1769	1799	1808–27	1829	1845	1859

Born on 14 September in Berlin

Lives in Paris, France

Publishes *Kosmos*, his major scientific work

Goes to South America with Bonpland

Travels across Russia and Siberia

Dies on 6 May

How did he die?

Von Humboldt died peacefully in Berlin at the age of 89.

South American travels

In 1799, Von Humboldt travelled to South America with French scientist Aimé Bonpland. They spent five years exploring and studying animals and plants. Among the highlights of his stay was a trip down the Orinoco River to study electric eels. In 1802, the two explorers climbed Mount Chimborazo in the Andes mountains. They climbed to 5,800 metres (19,119 feet), a world record at that time.

Back in Europe, von Humboldt's discoveries added greatly to geography and science. He investigated volcanoes, rocks, and ocean currents, one of which was named in his honour. He and Bonpland also collected and recorded thousands of new plant species.

Find out more

Read about von Humboldt's life at: http://geography.about.com/od/historyofgeography/a/vonhumboldt.htm

More information about von Humboldt and his travels can be found at: www.greatdreams.com/thor.htm

17

Mungo Park

Adventurous Scottish explorer Mungo Park succeeded in reaching the River Niger in Africa and mapping large parts of Africa before meeting a tragic and mysterious death.

What he said

66 ... The grand object of my mission – the long sought for majestic Niger, glittering in the morning sun... 99

How did he die?

No one knows if he was killed by an arrow or if he jumped into the Niger River and drowned.

Find out more

Take a look at this Scottish website to find out more about Park:
www.electricscotland.com/history/other/park_mungo.htm

Early life

The son of a farmer, Park was born near Selkirk, Scotland. He studied medicine and trained to be a surgeon. Later Park moved to London and got a job on a ship sailing for Asia. There, he was able to collect and study samples of the region's remarkable plants and animals.

Timeline

1771	1795	1799	1805	1806
Born in Scotland	First expedition to Africa	Publishes *Travels in the Interior of Africa*	Second expedition to Africa	Dies in Africa

African adventure

In 1795, Park embarked on an expedition to the River Niger in Africa. He reached Segou (in modern Mali) in July 1796 and became the first European to see the Niger. Back home, he wrote a best-selling book about his travels and became a doctor. But in 1805, he sailed for Africa again, hoping to follow the Niger to its source. The expedition was a disaster. One by one, his companions died and the rains made the going very slow. After following the river for more than 2,000 kilometres (1,250 miles), Park's canoe was attacked by hostile tribesmen and Park was killed. News of his death took several years to be confirmed.

Lewis and Clark

In 1804, the first overland expedition to cross the United States and reach the Pacific Ocean set out from St Louis, Missouri. Meriwether Lewis (right) and William Clark (left) led the expedition.

A good team

As a young man, Lewis joined the army, rising to the rank of captain. Then, in 1801, he became the president's private secretary. Two years later, the president chose Lewis to lead an expedition across Louisiana – part of the United States controlled by France at the time. Lewis picked his former army friend, William Clark, to go with him.

What they said

" This immense river so far as we have yet ascended, waters one of the fairest portions of the globe. "

Timeline

Clark born on 1 August

Set out from St Louis, Missouri

Lewis dies on 11 October

1770	1774	1804	1806	1809	1838

Lewis born on 18 August

Returns to St Louis, Missouri

Clark dies on 1 September

Find out more

Lots of interesting facts about Lewis and Clark can be found at:
www.lewisclark.net

Read about their travels at:
www.isu.edu/~trinmich/Discoverers.html

A fun site full of information:
http://perrybear.com/reporter/lewisandclark.html

Travelling west

In May 1804, Lewis and Clark set off from St Louis. They hoped to find an easy route to the Columbia River and on to the Pacific. On the way, they made friendly contacts with the local Indian people and hired an Indian guide, called Sacagawea. She led them across the Rocky Mountains – a difficult part of the journey. On the other side, however, lay the Columbia River. Finally, in December 1805, the two men reached the Pacific coast.

The following spring, Lewis and Clark began the long journey home. Back in St Louis, they were given a heroes' welcome. Their expedition was a great success. They had mapped large parts of unknown territory and returned with much information about the region's nature and people.

How did they die?

Lewis died of gunshot wounds on 11 October 1809. Clark died on 1 September 1838.

19

David Livingstone

One of the most famous explorers of the 19th century was Scottish **missionary** David Livingstone. His dream was to find the source of the River Nile.

What Stanley said to Livingstone

66 Dr Livingstone, I presume? 99

How did he die?

Livingstone died near Lake Bangwelu in Africa from malaria and dysentery.

Early life

Livingstone came from a poor family and had to work in a cotton mill from a young age. His family was very religious and felt that a good education was important. By saving hard, Livingstone was able to leave the mill and study medicine. He also became a missionary and, in 1840, was sent to Africa.

Timeline

1813	1841	1845	1866	1871	1873
Born on 19 March in Scotland		Marries Mary Moffat		Stanley finds Livingstone	
	Arrives in Africa for the first time		Sets off to look for the source of the Nile		Dies in May in Zambia

Quest for the Nile

Over 30 years, Livingstone explored Africa, visiting places no European had seen before. From 1852 to 1856, he crossed Africa from west to east, and became the first European to see the Victoria Falls.

In 1866, Livingstone set off to find the source of the River Nile. The expedition was a failure. Seriously ill, Livingstone was taken to the town of Ujiji on Lake Tanganyika, Tanzania. Back home, he was feared dead. In 1871, an American newspaper sent reporter Henry Morton Stanley to find him. He found him in Ujiji but could not persuade him to return home. In 1872, Livingstone made a second attempt to find the source of the Nile but died without achieving his goal.

Mary Kingsley

Mary Kingsley was one of the first famous women explorers. Fascinated by Africa, she travelled along rivers and through rainforests, living with local people.

Early life

Kingsley's childhood was spent looking after her mother, who was often ill. Her father was a doctor who travelled widely, and Kingsley was fascinated by his stories. When Kingsley's parents died in 1892, she decided to go to Africa to collect information for a book that her father had been writing about the life of the African people.

What she said

66 Never lose your head. 99

Timeline

1862	1892	1893	1895	1897	1900
Born in London on 13 October	Makes first journey to Africa		Writes *Travels in West Africa*		
	Kingsley's parents die	Second journey to Africa		Dies on 3 June in South Africa	

How did she die?

Kingsley died of typhoid in 1900. She had gone to South Africa to care for soldiers.

African adventure

Kingsley set sail from England in August 1893 and arrived in Luanda, Angola, a few weeks later. The trip went so well that two years later, she went back again. This time, the British Museum asked her to collect specimens of rare West African river fish. Kingsley canoed down the Ogowe River, deep into the rainforest. She wore a pair of her brother's trousers under her black skirt to keep off the leeches. Later, she spent several nights with the Fang, a tribe of cannibals.

Back in England, Kingsley spent the next three years giving lectures about the peoples of Africa. She also wrote a best-selling book, entitled *Travels in West Africa*.

Find out more

Read a detailed account of Kingsley's life at: http://africanhistory.about.com/library/weekly/aa011002a.htm

Find out about Kingsley at the Royal African Society's website: www.royalafricansociety.org

René Caillié

In 1828, French explorer, René Caillié, became the first European to reach the desert city of Timbuktu and return home alive.

What he said

66 ... I recall that at every halt, I fell to the ground from weakness, and had not even the strength to eat. 99

How did he die?

Caillié died in 1838 from a disease that he had caught during his African travels.

Early life

The son of a baker, Caillié was raised by his grandmother and left school early to work for a shoemaker. In his spare time, he read Daniel Defoe's book, *Robinson Crusoe*, and this inspired him to travel. In 1824, the Geographical Society of Paris offered a prize to the first explorer to travel to the desert city of Timbuktu in Senegal, Africa, and return alive. Caillié decided to take his chances.

Timeline

Born in France on 19 September	Sets out for Africa again	Publishes an account of his travels			
1799	**1817**	**1827**	**1828**	**1830**	**1838**
	First voyage to Senegal, Africa		Reaches Timbuktu	Dies in France in May	

Find out more

Read about the life of this great explorer at:
www.bookrags.com/biography/auguste-rene-caillie/

Find out more about Timbuktu at:
www.history.com/classroom/unesco/main.html

To Timbuktu

Caillié arrived in West Africa in March 1827. At that time, only Muslims were allowed into Timbuktu so Caillié learned Arabic and travelled in disguise. It was a long, risky journey. Half way through, Caillié fell ill and had to rest for five months. Finally, in April 1828, he reached Timbuktu.

To win the prize, Caillié still had to return home. He decided to take another route – across the Sahara Desert. Travelling by camel, he nearly died of thirst but still managed to reach France. As well as the prize, Caillié was given France's highest medal and a generous pension.

Sir Richard Burton

The English explorer, Richard Burton, was also a great scholar. Famous for his knowledge of other cultures, he spoke more than 20 languages.

Early life

Born in England, Burton was educated by tutors as his family travelled through Europe. He learned French, Italian, and Latin at an early age. A brilliant student, he later went to Oxford University but was thrown out for breaking the rules. Burton then joined the army and was sent to India.

What he said

66 Of the gladdest moments in human life, methinks is the departure upon a distant journey to unknown lands. 99

Timeline

Born in Devon, England, on 19 March

Locates Lake Tanganyika in Central Africa

Knighted by Queen Victoria

| 1821 | 1853 | 1858 | 1861 | 1886 | 1890 |

Travels to Makkah in Arabia

Marries Isabel Arundell

Dies in Trieste, Austria, on 20 October

Find out more

A site dedicated to the life of Burton and the books he wrote: http://burtoniana.org/

More information about Burton can be found at: www.bbc.co.uk/history/historic_figures/burton_sir_richard.shtml

Burton's travels

In 1853, Burton disguised himself as a Muslim and travelled to Makkah, the Islamic holy city. The city was forbidden to non-Muslims and Burton was lucky not to be killed. An expedition to Africa followed, during which he met fellow soldier and explorer, John Hanning Speke. In 1857, the two men travelled to East Africa hoping to find the source of the River Nile. Plagued by illness, they reached Lake Tanganyika in February 1858. Speke later discovered Lake Victoria and identified it as the source of the Nile.

Back at home, Burton and Speke quarrelled about Speke's findings. Speke later died in a hunting accident. Burton went on to become a **diplomat** in several countries. He also wrote a number of travel books and translated several books from other languages.

How did he die?

Burton died of a heart attack. He is buried in London in a tomb shaped like a Bedouin tent.

Burke and Wills

The first Europeans to cross Australia from south to north were Robert O'Hara Burke (left) and William Wills (right). Sadly, they died before they reached home.

What they said

❝ Nothing now but the greatest good luck can save any of us... ❞

How did they die?

Burke and Wills died from starvation and exposure to the sun at Cooper's Creek.

Preparing to leave

By the mid-19th century, British settlers had established towns along the coast of Australia. The centre of the continent was still a mystery, so the government of South Australia sent out an expedition to discover more. The leaders of the expedition were Burke and Wills.

Timeline

1821	1834	1852	1853	1860	1861
Burke born in Ireland		Wills emigrates to Australia		Burke and Wills chosen to lead expedition across Australia	
	Wills born in England		Burke emigrates to Australia		Burke and Wills die at Cooper's Creek

Across Australia

The expedition left Melbourne on 20 August 1860. By October, the party reached the town of Menindee where they then split up. Burke, Wills, John King, and Charles Gray pushed on to Cooper's Creek. Battling sand storms and scorching heat, the four men reached the Gulf of Carpentaria in the north of Australia the following February.

The journey back was dreadful. Gray died in April 1861. Weak with hunger and exhaustion, the other men made their way back to Cooper's Creek, only to find it abandoned. The support party they had asked to wait for them had left just a few hours before. Burke and Wills died in June. Months later, a rescue party found King still alive. He had been living with a group of **Aborigines**.

Gertrude Bell

English archaeologist Gertrude Bell left her comfortable life in London to explore the Middle East, becoming the first woman to cross the Arabian Desert.

Early life

Bell was born into a wealthy family from Durham, England. She went to Oxford University to study history when she was just 17 years old. After graduating, she went to Persia (modern-day Iran) to visit her uncle. She then spent the next 10 years travelling the world. During this time, Bell studied **archaeology** (ancient buildings and objects) and learned to speak several languages, including Arabic and Persian.

What she said

" The desert stretched away east and north and south, bathed in the soft splendour of the... sun. "

Did you Know?

Bell helped to found the Archaeological Museum in Baghdad, Iraq.

Timeline

Born in England on 14 July	Travels to Mesopotamia		Appointed Oriental Secretary in Baghdad
1868 1895	1909	1915	1920 1926
Goes to Oxford University	Works as an advisor in Cairo, Egypt		Dies on 12 July in Baghdad

To the Middle East

In 1899, Bell travelled to the Middle East and visited Palestine and Syria. She returned in 1905, when she met many local people and studied many ancient ruins. She travelled across the desert, recording her experiences in a book, *The Desert and the Sown*. Her account was the first that many people in Europe had ever heard about this region.

When the World War I broke out in 1914, Bell volunteered to work with the Red Cross in France. A year later, she was called back to the Middle East to advise the British rulers there. After the war, she continued to work in the newly formed country of Iraq.

Find out more

Read more about the life of this extraordinary female explorer at:
www.gerty.ncl.ac.uk

More information about Bell's life can be found at:
www.mnsu.edu/emuseum/information/biography/abcde/bell_gertrude.html

Sven Hedin

Swedish explorer and geographer, Sven Hedin, risked his life to cross the treacherous Takla Makan Desert in Central Asia – not once but twice.

What he said

66 My guiding principle was to explore only such regions where nobody else had been earlier. 99

Did you know?

He twice tried to reach the city of Lhasa in Tibet but was unsuccessful.

Find out more

Read about Hedin's life at:
www.iranica.com/articles/v12f2/v12f2006.html

Read Hedin's diary account of his expedition in the Takla Makan Desert:
www.iras.ucalgary.ca/~volk/sylvia/SvenHedin.htm

Early life

Hedin was born in Stockholm, Sweden. Even as a young boy, he wanted to be an explorer. After studying at the University of Stockholm, he got his first chance to travel when he took a post as a tutor at Baku on the Caspian Sea. Hedin later returned to Sweden to study geography and **geology**, but he was soon on the move again.

Timeline

Born in Sweden on 19 February		Attempts to reach Lhasa in Tibet		Dies on 26 November in Stockholm	
1865	**1894**	**1899–1902**		**1928–34**	**1952**
	Crosses the Takla Makan Desert in Central Asia			Leads the Sino-Swedish Expedition	

Difficulties in the desert

In 1893, Hedin set off on his greatest expedition. He travelled to Asia crossing mountainous regions in the middle of winter. Next, he set off across the Takla Makan Desert, with three local guides and eight camels. Things soon took a turn for the worse when the party ran out of water. They had been looking for the Khotan River but were unable to find it. Two of the men and all of the animals died. Hedin and his remaining companion struggled on, finally finding a life-saving waterhole.

Despite the journey, Hedin later re-crossed the desert. Back home, he gave lectures about his travels, wrote books and produced maps of the places he had visited.

Marc Aurel Stein

Hungarian-born archaeologist Marc Aurel Stein is famous for finding the "Caves of the Thousand Buddhas" in the Gobi Desert, Asia.

Desert discoveries

The "Caves of the Thousand Buddhas" were filled with ancient Buddhist manuscripts, wall paintings, and carvings. They had been preserved for centuries by the dry desert air.

Find out more

Read about Stein's journeys at:
www.monkeytree.org/
silkroad/stein.html

Take an online tour of the paintings in the caves at:
www.britishmuseum.org/explore
/online_tours/asia/cave_of_the_
1000_buddhas

Timeline

1862	1888	1907	1943
Born on 26 November in Budapest, Hungary	Takes a job at Punjab University in India	Discovers the "Caves of the Thousand Buddhas"	Dies on 26 October in Kabul, Afghanistan

Sir Wilfred Thesiger

In the 1940s, British explorer and writer Wilfred Thesiger crossed the legendary Rub 'al Khali ("Empty Quarter") of the Arabian Desert.

The Empty Quarter

Between 1946 and 1948, Thesiger twice made the journey across the Empty Quarter. He also spent five years with the Bedouin and wrote about them in his book, *Arabian Sands*.

Timeline

1910	1959	1995	2003
Born in Addis Ababa, Ethiopia, on 3 June	Publishes Arabian Sands	Awarded a knighthood	Dies in Surrey, England, on 24 August

Michel-Gabriel Paccard

In 1786, French doctor Michel-Gabriel Paccard became the first person to climb Mont Blanc. At 4,808 metres (15,775 feet), it is the highest peak in the Alps.

Alpine pioneer

On 8 August 1786, Paccard and mountain guide Jacques Balmat made it to the top after a gruelling, 14-hour climb. Suffering from **frostbite** and **snow blindness**, the two men then had to climb straight back down.

Find out more

Read an account of Paccard's Mont Blanc climb: www.jerberyd.com/climbing/stories/montblanc

Timeline

	Makes first attempt to climb Mont Blanc		Dies in Chamonix, France
1757	**1783**	**1786**	**1827**
Born in Chamonix, France		Reaches the summit of Mont Blanc	

Edward Whymper

Edward Whymper was a British artist who became a mountaineering legend. In 1865, he climbed the mighty Matterhorn, a mountain in the Swiss Alps.

Triumph and disaster

On 14 July 1865, after five unsuccessful attempts, Whymper and his party reached the summit (top peak) of the Matterhorn. He went on to explore Greenland and climbed many of the highest peaks in the Andes in South America.

Find out more

Discover more about Whymper's life at: www.powell-pressburger.org/Reviews/38_Challenge/Challenge01.html

Timeline

	Born in London on 27 April		Climbs Chimborazo in the Andes	
1840	**1865**	**1880**	**1911**
	Reaches the summit of the Matterhorn		Dies on 16 September

Hiram Bingham

Hiram Bingham became famous for rediscovering the long-lost **Inca** city of Machu Picchu in the Andes mountains.

Early life

Bingham was a brilliant student. He gained degrees from three American universities, and in 1907 he was appointed lecturer in South American history at Yale University. He later became a professor.

What he said

66 In the variety of its charms and the power of its spell, I know of no place in the world which can compare with it. 99

Timeline

Born in Hawaii on 19 November

Rediscovers Machu Picchu

Publishes *Lost City of the Incas*

1875 **1907** **1911** **1924–33** **1948** **1965**

Appointed lecturer at Yale University

Serves as a US politician

Dies on 6 June in Washington D.C., USA

Find out more

More information about Bingham and Machu Picchu can be found at: www.machupicchu.com

Read about Bingham's discovery of Machu Picchu at: www.nationalgeographic.co.uk/inca/machu_picchu_1.html

Find out about the history of Machu Picchu: www.andeantravelweb.com/peru/destinations/machupicchu/ruins.html

Long-lost city

In 1908, Bingham travelled to Peru for a scientific meeting. During his stay, he heard mysterious stories of ancient Inca cities in the Andes, which no one had seen for centuries. Excited by the thought of finding one of these cities, Bingham returned to Peru in 1911.

After weeks of searching, Bingham and his team had a stroke of luck. A local farmer told him about some Inca ruins on a nearby peak. The next day, Bingham made a dazzling discovery – the ruins of an ancient Inca fortress built more than 550 years ago. He named the city Machu Picchu because it was the name of the mountain on which it was built. Machu Picchu is now one of the world's major tourist attractions. Bingham went on to serve as a pilot in the US army and later became a politician.

Did you know?

Bingham wrote many books about his travels, including *Lost City of the Incas* (1948).

Hudson Stuck

In 1913, American explorer and missionary, Hudson Stuck, and three companions made the first ascent of Denali (Mount McKinley), in Alaska, the highest mountain in North America.

What he said

66 I would rather climb that mountain than own the richest gold mine in Alaska. 99

How did he die?

Stuck died from pneumonia at the age of 57.

Early life

Stuck emigrated to the United States when he was young. After graduating, he joined the Episcopal Church and became a minister. In 1905, he went to Alaska to teach about Christianity and spent the rest of his life there.

Timeline

Born in London on 11 November

Becomes archdeacon of the Yukon

Dies in Alaska on 10 October

1863   **1885**   **1905**   **1913**   **1920**

Emigrates to the United States

Reaches the summit of Denali

Climbing Denali

On 17 March 1913, Stuck and his three companions set off to climb Denali. The slightly lower North Peak of the mountain had already been reached three years earlier, so Stuck's team headed for the higher South Peak.

It was a gruelling climb. Blocks of ice as big as houses lay across their path. At one time, they had to stay in their tents because of a storm.

Around midday on 7 June, the four men finally reached the top. They spent two hours on the summit, taking measurements to work out the height of the mountain – 6,194 metres (20,322 feet). They also raised a small US flag made from two handkerchiefs. Stuck went on to write books about the historic climb, and about the peoples of Alaska.

Hillary and Tenzing

On 29 May 1953, Edmund Hillary (left) and Tenzing Norgay (right) became the first to reach the summit of Mount Everest. At 8,848 metres (29,029 feet), this is the highest place on Earth.

Early lives

Tenzing Norgay came from Nepal. He was a **Sherpa**, a group of people who live in the mountains of Nepal and know the conditions there well. He had made several attempts to climb Everest before 1953. Edmund Hillary worked as a bee-keeper but he took up climbing at school and later spent time in the **Himalayas**.

What they said

66 People do not decide to become extraordinary. They decide to accomplish extraordinary things. 99

Timeline

Tenzing born in Nepal	Tenzing and Hillary reach the summit of Everest	Hillary dies on 11 January in New Zealand	
1914	**1919**	**1953**	**1986**	**2008**
	Hillary born in New Zealand		Tenzing dies on 9 May in India	

Did you know?

Hillary and Norgay only stayed on the summit for 15 minutes because they were running out of oxygen.

On top of the world

In 1953, Norgay and Hillary joined the British Everest Expedition. Both were tough and determined, and made a good team. On 29 May, they left their final camp, some 8,370 metres (27,461 feet) up the mountain, and began their climb to the summit. Their goal was so close, but disaster struck. A rock, more than 12 metres (39 feet) high, blocked their path. Wedging himself into a crack in the rock, Hillary managed to haul himself up. Norgay followed. At last, at 11.30 a.m., they reached the summit.

When they returned, Hillary and Norgay received many honours and awards. Hillary continued to climb and took part in the British Commonwealth Antarctic Expedition to the South Pole. Norgay returned to India and ran a trekking company.

Find out more

Discover more about Hillary and Norgay's climb of Mount Everest at: http://imagingeverest.rgs.org

Find out why Hillary and Norgay were such important figures at: www.time.com/time/time100/heroes/profile/hillary_norgay01.html

Reinhold Messner

Reinhold Messner's achievement was to become the first person to climb all 14 of the world's highest peaks.

Climbing successes

In 1970, Messner climbed Nanga Parbat, in the Himalayas. He climbed Everest in 1978 for the first time without oxygen. In 1980, he became the first person to climb the mountain on his own. In 1986, he became the first person to climb all 14 of the world's highest peaks without a partner or team.

Find out more

Discover more about Messner's life and climbs at: www.jerberyd.com/ climbing/messner/

Timeline

Born in the South Tyrol, Italy		Climbs Everest solo	
1944	**1970**	**1978**	**1986**
	Climbs Everest without oxygen		Climbs the last of the world's highest peaks

Wanda Rutkiewicz

The great Polish climber Wanda Rutkiewicz was the first European woman to climb Mount Everest and the first woman ever to climb Mount K2.

A tragic story

After climbing Everest, Rutkiewicz scaled another seven of the world's highest peaks. She died in May 1992, trying to climb Mount Kangchenjunga, in Nepal. She was last seen at a height of over 8,000 metres (26,247 feet).

Find out more

Information about Rutkiewicz can be found at: www.everestnews.com/ history/wanda.htm

Timeline

	Climbs Mount Everest		Dies while climbing Kangchenjunga
1943	**1978**	**1986**	**1992**
Born in Poland on 4 February		First woman to climb K2	

Vitus Bering

Danish-born explorer Vitus Bering became the first European to see Alaska.

Early life

As a young man, Bering took to the seas as part of a voyage to the East Indies. Later, he joined the Russian Navy as an officer. It marked the beginning of a great career. In 1724, Bering was sent to explore the desolate, frozen wasteland of Siberia.

Siberian travels

Bering left St Petersburg, Russia, in 1725. In 1728, he led a dangerous expedition to find out whether Asia was joined to North America by land. He did sail through the Bering Strait, the stretch of water between the two continents, but fog prevented him from seeing land.

Did you know?

The Bering Strait, Bering Sea and the Bering Glacier are all named after Bering.

How did he die?

Bering died from **scurvy**, a disease caused by a lack of vitamin C.

Timeline

1681	1703	1725–30	1733	1741
Born in Denmark in August		Leads expedition across Siberia		Sets off on second expedition to Siberia
	Joins the Russian Navy		Organizes the Great Northern Expedition	Dies on 19 December

On a second expedition, in 1741, Bering once again set sail from Kamchatka and this time saw the snow-capped mountains of Alaska. Disaster struck on the return voyage. Bad weather forced Bering to spend the winter on an island (now called Bering Island) not far from the base in Kamchatka. Ill and exhausted, Bering and 28 of his men died.

Sir John Franklin

John Franklin was a British naval officer and experienced **Arctic** explorer. He disappeared while leading a daring expedition to discover the legendary **North-West Passage**.

What they said about him

66 HM ships *Terror* and *Erebus* were deserted on the 22nd April … Sir John Franklin died on 11th June 1847… 99

How did he die?

Franklin died soon after the ships became stuck in the ice near Baffin Bay.

Find out more

Discover more about Franklin at the English National Maritime Museum: www.nmm.ac.uk

A fun page full of information can be found at: www.collectionscanada.gc.ca/2/3/h3-1810-e.html

Early life

The son of a shopkeeper, Franklin persuaded his father to allow him to join the British Navy. He joined at the age of 14 and sailed on many voyages. He explored the coast of Australia and took part in two Arctic expeditions. In 1828, he was knighted by King George IV and later made governor of Tasmania.

Timeline

Born in England on 15 April		Second Arctic expedition	Governor of Tasmania, Australia		Dies on 11 June
1786	**1819**	**1823**	**1837–43**	**1845**	**1847**
	First expedition to the Arctic			Leads expedition to find North-West Passage	

The North-West Passage

In 1845, Franklin was asked to lead an expedition to the Arctic to look for the North-West Passage. This was a trade route that crossed the frozen north of North America. For centuries, European sailors had been searching for it. Franklin's plan was to sail north to Greenland, then head west.

By July, Franklin had reached Baffin Bay, but this was the last time they were seen. When news of his disappearance reached home, a huge rescue mission was launched. In 1859, a search party discovered a document revealing the ship had got stuck in ice. Some of the crew abandoned ship but died as they tried to find help.

Fridtjof Nansen

Norwegian explorer Fridtjof Nansen was the first person to cross Greenland on foot. Later, he sailed to the Arctic in a ship designed to resist the ice.

Early life

Nansen excelled in science and studied zoology at the University of Oslo in Norway. He was an excellent skier. In 1882, he made his first voyage to Greenland on a seal-hunting ship. He became fascinated with the icy world of the Arctic.

What he said

" Never stop because you are afraid – you are never so likely to be wrong. "

Timeline

Born in Norway on 10 October		Crosses Greenland on foot		Awarded the Nobel Peace Prize	
1861	**1882**	**1888**	**1893–96**	**1922**	**1930**
	Makes first voyage to Greenland		Sails to the Arctic in *Fram*		Dies in Norway on 13 May

Find out more

More information about Nansen can be found on the Nobel Prize website: www.nobelprize.org

Find out more about Nansen at: www.reisenett.no/norway/facts/history/nansen.html

Arctic explorations

In 1888, Nansen set off on his greatest adventure, crossing the island of Greenland from east to west. Back in Norway, he worked at the university and wrote several articles and books while he planned his next trip.

In 1893, he sailed for the Arctic in *Fram*, a ship built to withstand the crushing pressure of the ice. However, his ship became frozen in the ice, so Nansen and a companion tried to ski to the North Pole. They reached further north than anyone else but had to turn back. It was over a year before they saw *Fram* again.

Nansen returned to Norway and became involved in politics. He eventually won the Nobel Peace Prize in 1922 for his work in helping Russian **refugees**.

How did he die?

Nansen died peacefully on 13 May 1930 at his home outside Oslo, Norway.

Robert E. Peary

US Navy commander, Robert E. Peary, claimed to have been the first person to reach the North Pole on 6 April 1909.

What he said

66 The Pole at last! The prize of three centuries, my dream and ambition for 23 years. Mine at last…99

Did you know?

Peary's daughter, Marie, was born in the Arctic while his wife Josephine was on expedition with him.

Find out more

You'll find information and photographs at:
www.bowdoin.edu/arctic-museum

Find out more about Peary's explorations:
http://perrybear.com/reporter/peary.html

Early expeditions

In 1886, Peary made the first of a series of expeditions to the Arctic when he explored Greenland on a sledge pulled by dogs. He returned to map the north coast, proving that Greenland was an island. He also spent many months learning survival skills from the local **Inuit** people. Peary's dream was still to reach the North Pole. He made two attempts in 1902 and 1906, pushing further north.

Timeline

Born in Pennsylvania, USA, on 6 May

First expedition to Greenland

First attempt to reach the North Pole

Dies on 20 February

1865   **1881**   **1886**   **1902**   **1909**   **1920**

Joins US Navy

Reaches the North Pole on 6 April

To the North Pole

In 1908, he set off again, this time determined to reach his goal. Early the following year, from his base on Ellesmere Island, he sent support parties ahead to clear a trail and lay stores. Peary, his companion, Matthew Henson, and four Inuits then made a successful dash for the Pole.

Peary claimed that he had made it to the Pole and back to base in just 16 days. Some people doubted that he could have travelled so fast. There was also a rival claim from another American explorer, Frederick Cook. He reported that he had reached the Pole in 1908.

Roald Amundsen

One of the greatest polar explorers, Norwegian Roald Amundsen was the first person to reach the South Pole and navigate the North-West Passage for the first time.

Early life

His family were ship-owners but his mother wanted Amundsen to become a doctor. When she died, he left medicine for a life of exploration. Inspired by Franklin and Nansen, he set his sights on the Poles. From 1897 to 1899, Amundsen sailed to Antarctica and was forced to spend the freezing winter there when the ship got stuck in the ice. In 1903, he led the first expedition to navigate the North-West Passage in northern USA.

What he said

66 So we arrived and planted our flag at the geographical South Pole. Thanks be to God! 99

How did he die?

Amundsen died in 1928 when his plane crashed on a rescue mission in the Arctic.

Timeline

Born in Norway on 16 July	Leads first expedition to the South Pole	Dies around 18 June
1872	**1903–06**	**1910–12**	**1926**	**1928**
	Navigates the North-West Passage	Crosses the Arctic by airship	

To the South Pole

Amundsen was planning an attempt on the North Pole when he heard that Peary had reached it first. He decided to head south, knowing that British explorer Robert Scott (⇨p38) was already on his way. In October 1911, Amundsen's five-man team set off from the Bay of Whales in Antarctica. They arrived at the South Pole a month before Scott's group, on 14 December 1911.

Amundsen continued to explore right up to his death. In 1925, he flew a plane further north than anyone else. A year later, he crossed the Arctic in the airship *Norge*, making him the first person to have reached both poles.

Robert Scott

British explorer and navy captain Robert Scott led the second expedition to the South Pole in 1912. Tragically, his party died on their return journey.

Race to the Pole

Find out more

Discover more about Scott at:
www.south-pole.com

www.spri.cam.ac.uk/resources/kids/scott.html

Scott reached the South Pole on 17 January 1912, only to find that the Norwegian Roald Amundsen (⇨p37) had beaten him to it. They began the journey back to base but, sadly, they all died of frostbite and starvation on the way.

Timeline

1868	1901	1912
Born in England on 6 June	First expedition to Antarctica	Dies in Antarctica on 29 March / Reaches the South Pole on 17 January

Douglas Mawson

In 1911, Australian geologist Douglas Mawson led an expedition to Antarctica. Against the odds, he survived the journey, even though two of his companions died.

Survival story

Find out more

More information about Mawson can be found at:
www.south-pole.com

www.acn.net.au/articles/mawson/

Mawson struggled back to base alone, only to find that his ship had left a few hours before. Fortunately, a few men had stayed behind, and the group survived until the ship returned to rescue them.

Timeline

1882	1907	1911–14	1958
Born in England on 5 May	Joins the British Antarctic Expedition	Leads the Australasian Antarctic Expedition	Dies in Australia on 14 October

Ernest Shackleton

British explorer Ernest Shackleton had been to Antarctica twice when he faced his greatest challenge. His ship was crushed by the ice and he had to lead his crew to safety.

Early life

In 1901, Shackleton took part in the British National Antarctic Expedition, led by Robert Scott (⇨p38). Back in England, Shackleton tried to become a Member of Parliament but failed. In 1907, he returned to Antarctica, leading his own expedition. He got within 155 kilometres (96 miles) of the South Pole, closer than anyone else at that time.

What he said

  ❝ Men Wanted: For hazardous journey. Small wages, bitter cold, long months of complete darkness… ❞

Timeline

1874	1902	1907–09	1914–16	1921	1922

- Born in Ireland on 15 February
- Attempts to reach South Pole
- Second expedition to Antarctica
- *Endurance* expedition
- Sets out to sail around Antarctica
- Dies on South Georgia on 5 January

Find out more

Discover more about Shackleton at: www.south-pole.com

An account of Shackleton can be found at: www.bbc.co.uk/history/historic_figures/shackleton_ernest.shtml

A lucky escape

In 1914, Shackleton set out on his most daring trip. He wanted to cross Antarctica by dog sled. He set sail on his ship, *Endurance,* after months spent raising funds and finding a crew. Disaster struck when *Endurance* was crushed by the sea ice and had to be abandoned.

After spending several months camped on an ice floe (a floating piece of ice), Shackleton and his men managed to row in lifeboats to Elephant Island. But the island was so isolated that there was no hope of ever being rescued. Against the odds, Shackleton and five others sailed to South Georgia Island, more than 1,000 kilometres (620 miles) away. He later returned to Elephant Island to rescue his stranded men.

How did he die?

Shackleton died of a heart attack at the age of 47.

Salomon Andreé

Salomon Andreé was a Swedish engineer and Arctic explorer who met his death while attempting to reach the North Pole in a hot-air balloon.

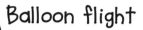

Balloon flight

On 11 July 1897, Andreé and his companions set off from the island of Spitsbergen in a balloon called the *Eagle*. They were never seen again. Their remains were found some 30 years later on White Island, not far from where they set off.

Timeline

Born in Sweden on 18 October		Dies on White Island in October
1854	**1897**	**1930**
	Attempts to fly to the North Pole	Andreé's remains found

Charles Lindbergh

Charles Lindbergh was an American pilot who became famous when he made the first solo non-stop flight across the Atlantic Ocean in his plane, the *Spirit of St Louis*.

Spirit of St Louis

In 1926, a prize of $25,000 was offered to the first person to fly non-stop from New York, USA, to Paris, France. Lindbergh took off from Roosevelt Airfield on 20 May 1927, arriving in Paris 33.5 hours later. He returned to a hero's welcome.

Find out more

More information can be found at:
www.charleslindbergh.com

www.allstar.fiu.edu/aerojava/lindbergh2.htm

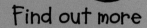

Timeline

	Trains as an army pilot		Dies in Hawaii on 26 August
1902	**1924**	**1927**	**1974**
Born in Detroit, USA, on 4 February		Flies solo across the Atlantic Ocean	

Amelia Earhart

An American pilot, Earhart was the first woman to fly solo across the Atlantic Ocean. She made many more record-breaking flights.

Early life

After leaving school, Earhart worked as a nurse in Toronto, Canada, looking after soldiers wounded in World War I. During this time, she visited an air fair and watched a flying display. She had her first plane ride in December 1920 and before long flying had become the most important thing in her life. Early in 1921, she had her first flying lesson, and later that year made her first solo flight.

What she said

66 Flying might not be all plain sailing, but the fun of it is worth the price. 99

Timeline

Born in Kansas, USA, on 24 July	Flies solo, non-stop across the Atlantic	Reported missing on 2 July
1897 **1928**	**1932** **1937**	**1937** **1939**
First woman to fly across the Atlantic	Sets off to fly around the world	Declared dead on 5 January

Find out more

Discover more about Earhart's life at: www.ameliaearhart.com

Look at the Amelia Earhart Museum's website for more information: www.ameliaearhartmuseum.org

Discover more on National Geographic's website: www.nationalgeographic.com/ngkids/9612/hart

Breaking records

In June 1928, Earhart became the first woman to fly across the Atlantic Ocean. She did not fly the plane but instead kept the flight log (diary). Back home, Earhart had become famous. She wrote a best-selling book, gave lectures, and helped to set up a club for women pilots. Then, in 1932, she became the first woman to fly solo across the Atlantic, from Newfoundland in Canada to Wales. In recognition, Earhart became the first woman to receive the Distinguished Flying Cross.

In March 1937, Earhart set off on her most daring adventure yet – to fly around the world at the **equator**, a feat never attempted before. Two-thirds of the way through the journey, Earhart's plane disappeared in the middle of the Pacific Ocean. She was never seen again.

Did you know?

Earhart was declared dead in 1939, two years after she went missing.

Yuri Gagarin

On 12 April 1961, Yuri Gagarin, became the first person in space when he blasted off in the *Vostok I* spacecraft.

What he said

66 I could have gone on flying through space forever. 99

How did he die?

Gagarin died in a plane crash while training to be a fighter pilot.

Find out more

Discover more about Gagarin at: http://russianarchives.com/gallery/gagarin/

NASA has further information about this great space explorer: www.nasa.gov/mission_pages/shuttle/sts1/gagarin_anniversary.html

Read a news article about Gagarin from 1961 at: http://century.guardian.co.uk/1960-1969/Story/0,6051,105531,00.html

Early life

The son of farm workers, Gagarin became interested in flying as a young boy. After leaving school, he worked in a steel foundry. He then studied engineering at the Saratov Technical School. He also joined a local flying club and learned to fly a light aircraft. Then, in 1955, he joined the Soviet Air Force. In 1959, he was interviewed for a "special project" and ordered to go to Moscow for medical tests. Gagarin did well in the tests that followed and was selected as a **cosmonaut**.

Timeline

Born in Russia on 9 March

Selected to train as a cosmonaut

Dies in Russia on 27 March

1934   **1955**   **1959**   **1961**   **1968**

Joins Soviet Air Force

Becomes first person in space

Into space

Early in April 1961, Gagarin was given the position of pilot of *Vostok I*, the first manned spacecraft. On 12 April 1961, he became the first person ever to fly in space. In a journey lasting 108 minutes, Gagarin **orbited** the Earth at a speed of 27,400 kilometres per hour (17,025 mph). This was three times faster than anyone had flown before. As *Vostok I* re-entered the Earth's atmosphere, Gagarin ejected and landed by parachute. He became a celebrity and travelled around the world, giving talks about his achievement.

Valentina Tereshkova

Russian cosmonaut, Valentina Tereshkova, became the first woman to go into space aboard *Vostok 6* on 16 June 1963.

Early life

Tereshkova was born into a poor family in Russia. Her father was a tractor driver, and her mother worked in a textile factory. After leaving school, Tereshkova worked in a textile factory and joined a local parachuting club. She made her first jump in 1959 aged 22. It was Tereshkova's interest in parachuting that led to her being selected as a cosmonaut. In 1961, the Soviet Union began a programme to send the first woman into space. Supervized by Yuri Gagarin, the selection process began later that year. Tereshkova and four others were chosen for training.

What she said

" Anyone who has spent any time in space will love it for the rest of their lives. "

Did you know?

Three days after returning from space, Tereshkova was declared a hero of the Soviet Union.

Timeline

1937	1959	1962	1963	1966	1969
Born in Russia on 6 March		Selected for cosmonaut training		Gets involved in politics	
	Makes first parachute jump		Becomes the first woman in space		Graduates as a cosmonaut engineer

Space flight

The five candidates enrolled into the Soviet Air Force and did the same training as the male cosmonauts. Of the five women, Tereshkova was the one chosen for the historic flight in *Vostok 6*, which blasted off on 16 June 1963. The flight lasted for almost three days. During this time, *Vostok 6* orbited the Earth 48 times. Tereshkova ejected from the capsule 6 kilometres (3¾ miles) above the ground and parachuted down. It was Tereshkova's only spaceflight. Almost 20 years passed before another woman journeyed into space.

Neil Armstrong

Neil Armstrong was an American **astronaut** who became the first person to walk on the Moon on 20 July 1969.

What he said

66 That's one small step for [a] man, one giant leap for mankind. 99

Did you know?

Armstrong carried out the first ever docking (joining) of two spacecraft in space.

Find out more

Further information about Armstrong can be found at:
www.jsc.nasa.gov/Bios/htmlbios/armstrong-na.html

More information and quotes about Armstrong can be read at:
www.tv.com/neil-armstrong/person/3458/trivia.html

Early life

Armstrong was interested in flying from an early age, and he gained his pilot's licence aged just 16. A year later, in 1947, Armstrong began studying **aeronautical engineering** at Purdue University, Indiana, USA. In 1949, Armstrong's studies were interrupted when the Navy called him up to train as a fighter pilot in the Korean War. He returned to Purdue in 1952 to complete his studies, and then became a civilian test pilot, flying the X-15 rocket plane.

Timeline

Born on 5 August in Ohio, USA

Fights in the Korean War

Becomes first person on the Moon on 20 July

1930	1946	1950–53	1962	1969	1978

Gains his pilot's licence

Selected as an astronaut

Receives the Congressional Space Medal of Honor

To the Moon

In 1962, Armstrong started astronaut training. Six years later, he became commander of *Apollo 11*, which was the first lunar landing mission.

At 9.32 a.m. on 16 July 1969, *Apollo 11* blasted off into space with Armstrong, Buzz Aldrin, and Michael Collins on board. Three days later, it went into orbit around the Moon. Armstrong and Aldrin crawled into *Eagle*, the **lunar module**. Collins continued to orbit the Moon. *Eagle* successfully landed on the surface of the Moon. Armstrong opened the hatch and began to climb down. He was later joined by Aldrin.

Buzz Aldrin

A few minutes after Neil Armstrong set foot on the surface of the Moon, he was joined by Buzz Aldrin, an astronaut who had already made a record-breaking spacewalk.

Early life

Born in New Jersey, USA, Aldrin graduated from the US Military Academy and served as a fighter pilot in the US Air Force during the Korean War. Aldrin flew 66 combat missions. After the war, Aldrin earned a **doctorate** in astronautics (the science of space flight) from the Massachusetts Institute of Technology.

What he said

" I think humans will reach Mars, and I would like to see it happen in my lifetime. "

Timeline

Born in New Jersey, USA, on 20 January

Named as pilot of *Gemini 12*

Retires from active duty

1930   **1963**   **1966**   **1969**   **1972**

Selected as an astronaut

Second person to walk on the Moon

Find out more

Read about Aldrin at:
www.buzzaldrin.com

NASA's biography of Aldrin:
www.jsc.nasa.gov/Bios/ htmlbios/aldrin-b.html

More information about Aldrin can be found at:
www.astronautix.com/astros/aldrin.htm

Space mission

Aldrin was selected for astronaut training in 1963. His first space flight came in 1966 when he was a pilot for *Gemini 12*, the last Gemini mission. On the four-day flight, Aldrin set a new record of 5.5 hours for a spacewalk and proved that astronauts could carry out work outside the spacecraft.

On 20 July 1969, Aldrin became the second person to walk on the Moon when he followed Neil Armstrong (⇨p44) out of the lunar module on to the Sea of Tranquility. The two men collected samples of Moon rock and dust, and carried out scientific experiments. They also set up an American flag on the Moon's surface. They had to stiffen the flag with wire because there is no wind on the Moon. Aldrin retired as an astronaut in 1972.

Did you know?

Since retiring, Aldrin has given lectures around the world, telling people about his experiences.

Glossary

Aborigines People who lived in Australia before the Europeans arrived there.

aeronautical engineering Design and building of machines that are flown in the air.

Antarctic Continent at the southern-most point of Earth.

apprentice Someone who works for a skilled person in order to learn a trade.

aqualung Equipment used by divers which allows them to breathe underwater.

archaeology Study of the past by looking at the remains of ancient buildings and objects.

Arctic Arctic Ocean and the lands around it.

astronaut Person who is trained for travelling in space.

astronomer Scientist who studies space, the stars and planets.

colonies Settlements made by people in countries other than their homeland.

cosmonaut Russian astronaut.

diplomat Person who represents a government in a foreign country.

doctorate Highest type of university degree.

dysentery Serious illness caused by drinking dirty water.

equator Imaginary line running around the middle of the Earth.

frostbite When parts of the body get so cold that they freeze and are destroyed.

geology Scientific study of Earth's rocks.

Himalayas Highest mountain range in the world. The Himalayas are found in Asia.

imperial Connected to an empire or an emperor.

Inca Connected to the Incas, an ancient people of South America.

Inuit People who have lived in the Arctic for thousands of years.

lunar module Space vehicle in which astronauts landed on the Moon.

Makkah City in Saudi Arabia, which is a holy place for Muslims.

malaria Killer disease caused by the bite of a particular kind of mosquito.

merchant Person who buys and sells goods.

missionary Person who works to try to make other people join their religion.

Mongols Warriors from Mongolia who invaded other lands in the 12th century.

navigation Skills used to plan the route of a vehicle, particularly a ship.

North-West Passage Sea route from Europe north-west across the top of North America.

orbit To travel around the Earth.

outlawed When a person is forced to leave a place because of a crime they have committed.

pilgrimage Journey to a place that is holy or special for another reason.

pilot Person who guides a ship or plane.

refugees People who have fled their homes because their lives are in danger.

scurvy Disease caused by a lack of vitamin C in the diet.

Sherpa Person from Nepal who is an expert in climbing mountains.

snow blindness Going blind for a while because of the light reflected off snow.

trading Buying and selling of goods between different people.

Index